A TASTE OF IRELAND

DISCOVER THE ESSENCE OF IRISH COOKING WITH 30 CLASSIC
RECIPES SHOWN IN 130 STUNNING PHOTOGRAPHS

BIDDY WHITE LENNON &
GEORGINA CAMPBELL

LORENZ BOOKS

This edition is published by Lorenz Books,
an imprint of Anness Publishing Ltd, Hermes House,
88–89 Blackfriars Road, London SE1 8HA;
tel. 020 7401 2077; fax 020 7633 9499

www.lorenzbooks.com; www.annesspublishing.com

If you like the images in this book and would like to investigate
using them for publishing, promotions or advertising, please visit
our website www.practicalpictures.com for more information.

UK agent: The Manning Partnership Ltd; tel. 01225 478444;
fax 01225 478440; sales@manning-partnership.co.uk
UK distributor: Grantham Book Services Ltd; tel. 01476 541080;
fax 01476 541061; orders@gbs.tbs-ltd.co.uk
North American agent/distributor: National Book Network;
tel. 301 459 3366; fax 301 429 5746; www.nbnbooks.com
Australian agent/distributor: Pan Macmillan Australia;
tel. 1300 135 113; fax 1300 135 103;
customer.service@macmillan.com.au
New Zealand agent/distributor: David Bateman Ltd;
tel. (09) 415 7664; fax (09) 415 8892

Publisher: Joanna Lorenz
Project Editor: Lucy Doncaster
Photographer: Craig Robertson
Food Stylist: Emma MacIntosh
Prop Stylist: Helen Trent
Designer: Nigel Partridge
Production Controller: Helen Wang

ETHICAL TRADING POLICY

At Anness Publishing we believe that business should be
conducted in an ethical and ecologically sustainable way, with
respect for the environment and a proper regard to the
replacement of the natural resources we employ.

As a publisher, we use a lot of wood pulp to make high-quality
paper for printing, and that wood commonly comes from spruce
trees. We are therefore currently growing more than 500,000
trees in two Scottish forest plantations near Aberdeen – Berrymoss
(130 hectares/320 acres) and West Touxhill (125 hectares/305
acres). The forests we manage contain twice the number of trees
employed each year in paper-making for our books.

Because of this ongoing ecological investment programme,
you, as our customer, can have the pleasure and reassurance of
knowing that a tree is being cultivated on your behalf to naturally
replace the materials used to make the book you are holding.

Our forestry programme is run in accordance with the UK
Woodland Assurance Scheme (UKWAS) and will be certified by
the internationally recognized Forest Stewardship Council (FSC).
The FSC is a non-government organization dedicated to
promoting responsible management of the world's forests.
Certification ensures forests are managed in an environmentally
sustainable and socially responsible basis. For further information
about this scheme, go to www.annesspublishing.com/trees

Material in this book has been previously published in
The Irish Heritage Cookbook

NOTES
Bracketed terms are intended for American readers.
For all recipes, quantities are given in both metric and imperial
measures and, where appropriate, in standard cups and spoons.
Follow one set of measures, but not a mixture, because they are
not interchangeable.
Standard spoon and cup measures are level. 1 tsp = 5ml,
1 tbsp = 15ml, 1 cup = 250ml/8fl oz.
Australian standard tablespoons are 20ml. Australian readers
should use 3 tsp in place of 1 tbsp for measuring small quantities.
American pints are 16fl oz/2 cups. American readers should use
20fl oz/2.5 cups in place of 1 pint when measuring liquids.
Electric oven temperatures in this book are for conventional ovens.
When using a fan oven, the temperature will probably need to be
reduced by about 10–20°C/20–40°F. Since ovens vary, you should
check with your manufacturer's instruction book for guidance.
The nutritional analysis given for each recipe is calculated per
portion (i.e. serving or item), unless otherwise stated. If the recipe
gives a range, such as Serves 4–6, then the nutritional analysis will
be for the smaller portion size, i.e. 6 servings. Measurements for
sodium do not include salt added to taste.
Medium (US large) eggs are used unless otherwise stated.

Front cover shows Potato Cakes – for recipe, see page 10.

contents

introduction

With its stunning coastline, lush, verdant countryside and lively towns and cities, Ireland has a rich and diverse culinary history and is home to a wide range of delectable and much-loved classic dishes that span the divide between the Republic of Ireland in the south and Northern Ireland to the north.

It is often said that Ireland does not have a climate; it has weather. For a small island this is extremely varied, changing from sunshine to rain within minutes, although the rainfall is not normally excessive.

In these showery conditions, humidity tends to be high, resulting in cloud cover and less bright sunshine than in much of Europe.

Despite the lack of sunshine, Ireland is a fast-growing food-exporting nation, with its tender grass-fed beef and lamb and top-quality dairy produce selling all over the world. Similar foodstuffs are produced everywhere on the island, although the topography of some regions – such as the mountains of Connemara and Wicklow, which are famous for their lamb – makes them better suited to producing specific foods.

The Irish value locally produced goods and celebrate the country's regional foods. Among the many favourite ingredients are native Irish oysters, exquisite hams, sausages and black puddings (blood sausages), tender cuts of mountain lamb or kid, beef from centuries-old

Above: Irish cattle produce some of the best beef in the world.
Left: The stunning coast of Ireland abounds with fish and shellfish.

cattle breeds, flavoursome game, many different types of potato, artisan farmhouse cheeses, succulent soft fruits and much more.

These indigenous foods are then transformed into an array of mouthwatering classic dishes, following traditional recipes that have been handed down from generation to generation, or are combined with ingredients and techniques from abroad to give an innovative twist to the national dishes.

Prevented by the climate from making wine, the Irish have become expert brewers of ciders and beers. Following the arrival of the secret art of distillation from the Mediterranean, whiskey (*uisce beatha* – "the water of life") is also produced and remains a key industry.

This beautiful little book provides an inspiring introduction to the delectable dishes that make up the Irish cuisine. From warming soups and delicate appetizers to

Above left: Ireland is bounded by fertile waters and has good conditions for growing crops.
Top: Irish whiskey is made in traditional distilleries across Ireland.
Above: Ancient breeds of upland sheep provide wonderful local meat.

satisfying main courses, flavoursome side dishes and a range of sweet treats, the traditional recipes reveal the very best that Ireland has to offer in one delightful volume.

breakfasts

A traditional Irish cooked breakfast is far
more than the sum of its parts. Bacon,
sausages, mushrooms, tomato and egg
are the basic ingredients, and you can use
them all, or a selection if preferred. Freshly
squeezed juice or fruit begin the feast, then
yogurt, cereals or porridge herald the hot
plate. Home-baked bread and preserves
accompany – and all is washed down with
tea or coffee. No wonder lunch is so often
off the menu for visitors to Ireland!

Left: The traditional Irish cooked breakfast is a
great way to start the day and is often enjoyed
as part of a lazy weekend brunch.

boxty potato pancakes

Said to have originated during the Irish famine, these pancakes use blended potatoes in the batter mix and can be made as thin or thick as you like. They are delicious rolled around a filling such as cabbage and bacon in a light mustard sauce.

3 Heat a little butter on a griddle or cast-iron frying pan. Pour about a quarter of the mixture into the pan – if the consistency is right it will spread evenly over the base.

4 Cook over a medium heat for about 5 minutes on each side, depending on the thickness of the cake. Serve rolled with your chosen filling.

Makes 4

450g/1lb potatoes, peeled
 and chopped
50–75g/2–3oz/½–⅔ cup plain
 (all-purpose) flour
about 150ml/¼ pint/⅔ cup milk
salt to taste
knob (pat) of butter

1 Place the potatoes in a blender or food processor and process until the potato is liquidized (blended).

2 Add the flour and enough milk to give a dropping consistency, and add salt to taste. The milk and flour can be adjusted, depending on how thin you like your pancake.

Per portion Energy 163Kcal/689kJ; Protein 4.8g; Carbohydrate 30.9g, of which sugars 2.7g; Fat 3.1g, of which saturates 1.7g; Cholesterol 8mg; Calcium 69mg; Fibre 1.9g; Sodium 236mg

oatmeal pancakes with bacon

These oaty pancakes have a special affinity with rashers of good, dry-cured bacon, making an interesting alternative to the big traditional fry-up. Serve with best-quality or home-made sausages, fried or poached eggs and cooked tomatoes.

Makes 8

115g/4oz/1 cup fine wholemeal
  (whole-wheat) flour
25g/1oz/¼ cup fine pinhead oatmeal
pinch of salt
2 eggs
300ml/½ pint/1¼ cups buttermilk
butter or oil, for greasing
8 bacon rashers (strips)

1 Mix the flour, oatmeal and salt in a bowl or food processor, beat in the eggs and add enough buttermilk to make a creamy batter.

2 Heat a griddle or cast-iron frying pan over a medium-hot heat. When very hot, grease lightly with butter or oil. Pour in the batter, about a ladleful at a time.

3 Tilt the pan around to spread evenly and cook for about 2 minutes on the first side, or until set and the underside is browned. Turn over and cook for 1 minute until browned.

4 Keep the pancake warm while you cook the others. Fry the bacon. Roll the pancakes with a cooked rasher to serve.

Per portion Energy 202Kcal/845kJ; Protein 11.9g; Carbohydrate 13.1g, of which sugars 2g; Fat 11.8g, of which saturates 4.8g; Cholesterol 87mg; Calcium 59mg; Fibre 1.5g; Sodium 654mg

potato cakes

This is the traditional method of making potato cakes on a griddle or in a heavy frying pan. The cakes are usually buttered and eaten hot with sugar. Commercial versions are available throughout Ireland as thin, pre-cooked potato cakes, which are then fried.

Makes about 8

675g/1½lb potatoes, peeled
  and chopped
25g/1oz/2 tbsp unsalted
  (sweet) butter
about 175g/6oz/1½ cups plain
  (all-purpose) flour
salt
butter and sugar, to serve (optional)

1 Boil the potatoes in a large pan until tender, then drain well and mash. Salt well, then mix in the butter and allow to cool a little.

2 Turn out on to a floured work surface and knead in about one-third of its volume in flour, or as much as is needed to make the dough pliable. Avoid overhandling.

3 Roll out the dough to a thickness of about 1cm/½in and cut into small, equal-sized triangles.

4 Heat a dry griddle or heavy frying pan over a low heat and cook the potato cakes in batches on it for about 3 minutes on each side until browned. Serve hot with butter, or sugar, if you like.

Per portion Energy 1276Kcal/5392kJ; Protein 30.4g; Carbohydrate 249.1g, of which sugars 6.7g; Fat 24.1g, of which saturates 13.4g; Cholesterol 53mg; Calcium 282mg; Fibre 14g; Sodium 203mg

jugged kippers

The demand for naturally smoked kippers is ever increasing. Excellent examples are those from the Woodcock Smokery in West Cork. They are popular for breakfast, served with scrambled eggs or with soda bread or toast and a wedge of lemon.

Serves 4

4 kippers (smoked herrings), whole
   or filleted
25g/1oz/2 tbsp butter
ground black pepper

Cook's tip
Jugging is the same as poaching using just a jug (pitcher) and kettle.

1 Select a large heatproof jug (pitcher) that is tall enough for the kippers to be completely immersed when the water is added.

2 If the heads are still on the fish, remove them using a sharp knife and discard.

3 Put the fish into the jug, tails up, and then cover them with boiling water. Leave for about 5 minutes, until tender.

4 Drain well and serve on warmed plates with a knob (pat) of butter and a little black pepper on each kipper.

Per portion Energy 449Kcal/1859kJ; Protein 31.8g; Carbohydrate 0g, of which sugars 0g; Fat 35.7g, of which saturates 8.3g; Cholesterol 123mg; Calcium 96mg; Fibre 0g; Sodium 1.5g

the traditional Irish breakfast

A hearty Irish cooked breakfast was once eaten almost every day, but today it is normally reserved for weekend brunches and lazy holiday breakfasts. The beauty of the dish is that you can choose whichever ingredients you like, tailoring the meal to your own tastes. Just ensure that you use the very best quality.

Serves 4

4 lamb's kidneys, halved
  and trimmed
wholegrain mustard, for spreading
8 rashers (strips) back or streaky
  (fatty) bacon, preferably dry-cured
275g/10oz black pudding (blood
  sausage), sliced
225g/8oz good quality sausages
butter or oil, for grilling or frying
sea salt and ground black pepper
4 tomatoes, halved
4–8 flat field (portabello) mushrooms
4 potato cakes or potato bread
4 eggs
chopped fresh chives or fresh
  parsley sprigs, to garnish

1 Spread the kidneys with a little mustard. Grill (broil) or fry the bacon, black pudding, kidneys and sausages in a large frying pan with butter or oil, as preferred, until the bacon is crisp and everything is nicely browned. Season to taste, and then keep warm.

2 Meanwhile, fry or grill the halved tomatoes with knobs (pats) of butter, and fry or bake the flat field mushrooms, preferably in the juices from the bacon, kidneys and sausages, until they are just tender.

3 Fry the potato cakes or potato bread until warmed through and golden brown on both sides.

4 Cook the eggs to your liking. Arrange everything on large, warm plates, and garnish with chopped chives or parsley sprigs. Serve at once.

Variation

Although kidneys and black pudding (blood sausage) are an integral part of the traditional Irish breakfast, you can of course omit them if you don't like them.

Per portion Energy 894Kcal/3728kJ; Protein 50.6g; Carbohydrate 40.1g, of which sugars 5.5g; Fat 60.4g, of which saturates 20.1g; Cholesterol 618mg; Calcium 115mg; Fibre 3.5g; Sodium 2.25mg

soups and appetizers

Soups and broths (brotchán) hold an honoured position in traditional Irish cooking. Originally a simple but nourishing gruel made with oatmeal and vegetables, typical Irish soups later developed into the "meal in a soup bowl" that uses a wide variety of vegetables, fish and meat. Although appetizers are not a traditional way to begin an Irish family meal, they have become increasingly popular and today many would cite these tasty little dishes as their favourite part of a larger meal.

Left: Hearty Seafood Chowder can be made with whatever fish and shellfish is available and served with brown bread to make a satisfying meal.

brotchán foltchep

This traditional leek and oatmeal soup is also known as Brotchán Roy and combines leeks, oatmeal and milk – three ingredients that have been staple foods in Ireland for centuries. Serve with freshly baked bread and Irish butter.

Serves 4–6

about 1.2 litres/2 pints/5 cups
   chicken stock and milk, mixed
30ml/2 tbsp medium pinhead
   oatmeal
25g/1oz/2 tbsp butter
6 large leeks, sliced into
   2cm/¾ in pieces
sea salt and ground black pepper
pinch of ground mace
30ml/2 tbsp chopped fresh parsley
single (light) cream and chopped
   fresh parsley or chives, to garnish

1 Bring the stock and milk mixture to the boil in a large pan over medium heat and sprinkle in the oatmeal. Stir well to prevent lumps forming, and then simmer gently.

2 Thoroughly wash the leeks in a bowl, ensuring that no dirt or grit remains. Melt the butter in a separate pan and cook the leeks over a gentle heat until softened slightly, then add them to the stock mixture.

3 Simmer for a further 15–20 minutes, or until the oatmeal is cooked. Extra stock or milk can be added if the soup is too thick.

4 Season with salt, pepper and mace, stir in the parsley and serve in warmed bowls. Decorate with a swirl of cream and some chopped fresh parsley or chives, if you like.

Cook's tip

It is very important that you wash the leeks properly, as any remaining dirt or grit will spoil the soup.

Variation

Make nettle soup in the spring, when the nettle tops are young and tender. Strip about 10oz/275g nettle tops from the stems, chop them and add to the leeks. Continue as above.

Per portion Energy 199Kcal/834kJ; Protein 10g; Carbohydrate 19.5g, of which sugars 12.4g; Fat 9.6g, of which saturates 5.1g; Cholesterol 22mg; Calcium 243mg; Fibre 5.8g; Sodium 219mg

seafood chowder

This satisfying fish soup is infinitely adaptable according to the availability of fresh
fish and shellfish. Hand around freshly made brown bread separately.

Serves 4–6

50g/2oz/¼ cup butter
1 large onion, chopped
115g/4oz bacon, rind removed, diced
4 celery sticks, diced
2 large potatoes, diced
450g/1lb ripe tomatoes, chopped or
    400g/14oz can chopped tomatoes
about 450ml/¾ pint/2 cups fish stock
450g/1lb white fish fillets, such as
    cod, plaice, flounder or haddock,
    skinned and cut into small chunks
225g/8oz shellfish, such as prawns
    (shrimp), scallops, cockles or mussels
about 300ml/½ pint/1¼ cups milk
25g/1oz/¼ cup cornflour (cornstarch)
sea salt and ground black pepper
cream and chopped parsley,
    to garnish

1 Melt the butter in a large pan and stir in the onion, bacon, celery and potatoes.
Cover and cook over very gentle heat for 5–10 minutes, without colouring.

2 Purée the tomatoes in a blender, and sieve (strain) them to remove the skin
and pips. Add to the pan along with the fish stock. Bring to the boil, cover and
simmer until the potatoes are tender, skimming the top occasionally as required.

3 Prepare fresh prawns by plunging briefly into a pan of boiling water. Remove
from the pan as the water boils. Cool and peel.

4 If using cockles or mussels, scrub the shells and discard any that don't open
when tapped. Put into a shallow, heavy pan. Cover and cook over a high heat
for a few minutes, shaking occasionally, until they have all opened. Discard any
that fail to open. Remove from their shells. Raw shelled scallops can be left whole.

5 Add the shellfish to the soup. Blend the milk and cornflour together in a
small jug (pitcher), stir into the soup and bring to the boil again. Reduce the
heat, and cover and simmer for a few minutes until the fish is just tender.
Adjust the texture with milk or stock, if necessary, and season to taste. Serve
in warm soup bowls, garnished with a swirl of cream and some parsley.

Per portion Energy 488Kcal/2050kJ; Protein 46g; Carbohydrate 36.2g, of which sugars 11.3g; Fat 18.7g, of which saturates 9.6g; Cholesterol 127mg; Calcium 163mg; Fibre 3.5g; Sodium 771mg

kidney and bacon soup

Although there is a modern twist in the seasonings, the two main ingredients of this meaty soup are still very traditionally Irish.

Serves 4–6

225g/8oz ox kidney
15ml/1 tbsp vegetable oil
4 streaky (fatty) bacon rashers
  (strips), chopped
1 large onion, chopped
2 garlic cloves, finely chopped
15ml/1 tbsp plain (all-purpose)
  flour
1.5 litres/2½ pints/6¼ cups water
a good dash of Worcestershire
  sauce
a good dash of soy sauce
15ml/l tbsp chopped fresh thyme,
  or 5ml/1 tsp dried thyme
75g/3oz/¾ cup grated cheese
4–6 slices French bread,
  lightly toasted
salt and ground black pepper

1 Wash the kidney in cold, salted water. Drain, dry well on kitchen paper and chop into small pieces.

2 Heat the vegetable oil in a large pan over a medium heat. Add the chopped streaky bacon and sauté for a few minutes. Add the prepared kidney and continue cooking until nicely browned.

3 Stir in the chopped onion and chopped garlic, and cook until the onion is just soft – do not let it brown.

4 Add the flour and cook for 2 minutes. Gradually add the water, stirring constantly. Add the sauces, thyme and seasoning to taste. Reduce the heat and simmer gently for 30–35 minutes.

5 Sprinkle the cheese on to the French bread and grill (broil) until it is bubbling. Pour the soup into bowls, and top with the toast.

Variation

You can omit the slices of toasted French bread with cheese on and just serve this hearty soup with soda bread and butter, if you prefer.

Per portion Energy 445Kcal/1866kJ; Protein 26.8g; Carbohydrate 40.7g, of which sugars 5.4g; Fat 20.2g, of which saturates 8.1g; Cholesterol 192mg; Calcium 241mg; Fibre 2.4g; Sodium 1.18g

black pudding with potato and apple

Black pudding has come a long way from its once humble position in traditional Irish cooking. Made in West Cork and widely available, Clonakilty black pudding is especially popular, and features on many a contemporary restaurant menu.

4 Cut the apple into wedges, add to the pan and sauté until golden brown. Add the vinegar, and boil up the juices. Stir in the butter and season.

5 Cut the potato cake into wedges and divide among four plates. Arrange the black pudding and mushrooms on top, pour over the apples and the juices and serve immediately.

Serves 4

4 large potatoes, peeled
45ml/3 tbsp olive oil
salt and ground black pepper
8 slices of black pudding (blood sausage), such as Clonakilty
115g/4oz cultivated mushrooms, such as oyster or shiitake
2 eating apples, peeled and cored
15ml/1 tbsp sherry or wine vinegar
15g/1oz/2 tbsp butter

1 Grate the potatoes, then drain and squeeze out the excess moisture.

2 Heat 30ml/2 tbsp olive oil in a frying pan, add the potatoes and season. Press into the pan with your hands. Cook until browned, then turn over and cook the other side. Keep warm.

3 Heat the remaining oil and sauté the black pudding and mushrooms for 2 minutes. Remove and keep warm.

Per portion Energy 247Kcal/1034kJ; Protein 4.2g; Carbohydrate 28.8g, of which sugars 5.4g; Fat 13.6g, of which saturates 4g; Cholesterol 13mg; Calcium 16mg; Fibre 2.4g; Sodium 132mg

oysters on the half-shell

The best native Irish oysters come from the Galway area on the west coast and, every September, festivals are held in Galway and Clarenbridge to celebrate the beginning of the new season. Enjoy the oysters with freshly made brown soda bread.

Serves 2–4

24 Galway oysters, in the shell
crushed ice and dulse or dillisk
   (soaked if dried), to garnish
lemon wedges, to serve

1 Insert the end of an oyster knife between the shells near the hinge and work until you cut through the muscle.

2 Catch the liquid in a bowl. When the oysters are open, discard the shells.

3 Divide the oysters, in the deep halves, among four plates lined with crushed ice and soaked dulse.

4 Strain the reserved oyster liquid over the oysters. Serve with the lemon wedges.

Cook's tip

Although they were once plentiful, Galway oysters are now a delicacy and are usually eaten raw. It is important that you buy them with their shells tightly clamped together, showing that they are still alive. The edible seaweed, dulse, or dillisk, as it is also known, is an appropriate garnish for oysters.

Per portion Energy 78Kcal/330kJ; Protein 13g; Carbohydrate 3.3g, of which sugars 0g; Fat 1.6g, of which saturates 0.3g; Cholesterol 68mg; Calcium 168mg; Fibre 0g; Sodium 612mg

smoked Wicklow trout with cucumber

Rainbow trout is farmed in the Wicklow Hills and the smoked trout fillets are widely available in vacuum packs in supermarkets. They need no further cooking or preparation unless you require an accompanying salad or sauce, making them an excellent fresh convenience food and a deservedly popular cold first course or light meal. Allow one or two smoked trout fillets per person.

Serves 4

1 small cucumber
4–8 smoked trout fillets
sprigs of dill, to garnish
brown bread and butter,
    to serve

For the dressing
90ml/6 tbsp extra virgin olive oil
30ml/2 tbsp white wine vinegar
15ml/1 tbsp finely chopped
    fresh dill
sea salt and ground
    black pepper

1 To make the dressing, whisk the oil and vinegar together vigorously in a small bowl, or shake in a screw-top jar.

2 Finely chop the dill, then blend into the dressing and season with salt and ground black pepper to taste.

3 Peel the cucumber, if you prefer, and slice it thinly. Arrange with the trout fillets on four serving plates.

4 Sprinkle the fish with the dressing, and garnish with sprigs of dill. Serve with brown bread and butter.

Variation
The cucumber salad can be made up beforehand, if you prefer, allowing the cucumber slices to marinate in the dressing.

Per portion Energy 467Kcal/1943kJ; Protein 55g; Carbohydrate 0.7g, of which sugars 0.6g; Fat 27g, of which saturates 4.7g; Cholesterol 226mg; Calcium 92mg; Fibre 0.3g; Sodium 206mg

main courses

As an island nation, the Irish prize the wide range of fabulous fish and shellfish on offer and use them to make delectable dishes, such as Mackerel with Rhubarb Sauce or Crab Bake. Meat and poultry also play an important role, with pork, beef and lamb taking star turns in many family meals. Wild game, both furred and feathered, has always been plentiful in Ireland and, in addition to supplies of farmed produce such as rabbit, is still available in season.

Left: Main courses in Ireland tend to be well-balanced meals comprising simply cooked protein accompanied by potatoes and vegetables.

stuffed white fish wrapped in bacon

Caught mainly off the east coast of Ireland, white fish such as whiting and lemon sole, plaice and flounder are especially good for this recipe, which includes strong flavours such as bacon and parsley. Serve with new potatoes and vegetables.

Serves 4

4 good-size or 8 small fish fillets, such as whiting, lemon sole, plaice or flounder
4 streaky (fatty) bacon rashers (strips)
boiled new potatoes and green beans or broccoli, to serve

For the stuffing
50g/2oz/¼ cup butter
1 onion, finely chopped
50g/2oz/1 cup fine fresh brown breadcrumbs
5ml/1 tsp finely chopped fresh parsley
a good pinch of mixed dried herbs
sea salt and ground black pepper

1 Preheat the oven to 190°C/375°F/Gas 5. Trim the fish fillets. If they are fairly big, cut them in half lengthways; leave small ones whole. Remove the rind and any gristle from the streaky bacon rashers.

2 To make the stuffing, melt the butter in a small pan, add the onion and cook gently until softened but not browned. Add the breadcrumbs, parsley and herbs. Season to taste.

3 Divide the stuffing between the fillets, roll them up and wrap a bacon rasher around each one.

4 Secure the stuffed fish and bacon rolls firmly with wooden cocktail sticks (toothpicks) and lay them in a single layer in the base of a shallow buttered baking dish. Cover the dish with foil and bake in the preheated oven for 15 minutes, removing the cover for the last 5 minutes to allow the bacon to brown.

5 Serve the fish rolls immediately with boiled new potatoes and green beans or broccoli.

Per portion Energy 344Kcal/1436kJ; Protein 38.1g; Carbohydrate 12.5g, of which sugars 2.4g; Fat 15.9g, of which saturates 8.2g; Cholesterol 120mg; Calcium 44mg; Fibre 0.8g; Sodium 662mg

mackerel with rhubarb sauce

Mackerel are available in Ireland for most of the year, but they are really at their best in early summer, just when rhubarb is growing strongly – a happy coincidence, as the tartness of rhubarb offsets the richness of the oily fish to perfection.

Serves 4

4 whole mackerel, cleaned
25g/1oz/2 tbsp butter
1 onion, finely chopped
90ml/6 tbsp fresh white breadcrumbs
15ml/1 tbsp chopped fresh parsley
finely grated rind of 1 lemon
freshly grated nutmeg
1 egg, lightly beaten
melted butter or olive oil, for brushing
sea salt and ground black pepper

For the sauce

225g/8oz rhubarb (trimmed weight),
   cut into 1cm/½in lengths
25–50g/1–2oz/2–4 tbsp sugar
25g/1oz/2 tbsp butter
15ml/1 tbsp chopped fresh tarragon

1 Ask the fishmonger to bone the mackerel, or do it yourself: open out the body of the cleaned fish, turn flesh side down on a board and run your thumb firmly down the backbone – when you turn the fish over, the bones should lift out in one complete section.

2 Melt the butter in a pan and cook the onion gently for 5–10 minutes, until softened but not browned. Add the breadcrumbs, parsley, lemon rind, salt, pepper and grated nutmeg. Mix well, and then add the beaten egg to bind.

3 Divide the mixture between the four fish, wrap the fish over and secure with cocktail sticks (toothpicks). Brush with melted butter or olive oil. Preheat the grill (broiler) and cook under a medium heat for about 8 minutes on each side.

4 Meanwhile, make the sauce: put the rhubarb into a pan with 75ml/2½fl oz/ ⅓ cup water, 25g/1oz/2 tbsp of the sugar and the butter. Cook over a gentle heat until the rhubarb is tender. Taste for sweetness and add extra sugar if necessary, bearing in mind that the sauce needs to be quite sharp.

5 Serve the stuffed mackerel with the hot sauce garnished with the tarragon.

Per portion Energy 728Kcal/3034kJ; Protein 48.2g; Carbohydrate 27.5g, of which sugars 9.8g; Fat 48g, of which saturates 14.3g; Cholesterol 193mg; Calcium 129mg; Fibre 1.8g; Sodium 398mg

crab bake

Plentiful all around the Irish coast, crabs are popular on bar menus. Cork Dry Gin, which is made in Midleton, County Cork, brings an extra dimension to this delicious dish. Serve hot with rice, or fresh crusty bread, and a side salad.

Serves 2

225g/8oz cooked white crab meat
juice of ½ lemon
15ml/1 tbsp chopped fresh herbs
20ml/4 tsp Cork Dry Gin
5ml/1 tsp smooth Dijon mustard
5ml/1 tsp wholegrain Dijon mustard
60ml/4 tbsp grated hard cheese
ground black pepper

For the béchamel sauce
1 small onion
3 cloves
300ml/½ pint/1¼ cups milk
1 bay leaf
25g/1oz/2 tbsp butter
25g/1oz/¼ cup plain
   (all-purpose) flour

1 First make an infusion for the béchamel sauce: stud the onion with the cloves, and then put it into a small pan with the milk and bay leaf. Bring slowly to the boil, then allow to infuse (steep) for 15 minutes, and strain.

2 Preheat the oven to 180°C/350°F/Gas 4 and butter two large gratin dishes. Toss the crab meat in the lemon juice. Divide it between the dishes and add a pinch of herbs to each. Sprinkle each dish with 5ml/1 tsp gin and pepper.

3 Melt the butter for the sauce in a pan, stir in the flour and cook over a low heat for 1–2 minutes. Gradually add the infused milk, stirring constantly to make a smooth sauce. Simmer over a low heat for 1–2 minutes.

4 Blend the béchamel sauce with the two mustards and use to cover the crab. Sprinkle the cheese on top, and bake for 20–25 minutes, or until hot and bubbling. Serve immediately.

Cook's tip
The recipe can also be divided between four smaller gratin dishes to serve four as a first course.

Per portion Energy 224Kcal/936kJ; Protein 17.4g; Carbohydrate 9.6g, of which sugars 4.5g; Fat 11.9g, of which saturates 7.4g; Cholesterol 73mg; Calcium 282mg; Fibre 0.4g; Sodium 489mg

mustard baked chicken

In this simple recipe, chicken pieces are flavoured with tarragon and a mild, aromatic wholegrain mustard. Speciality mustards, such as this whiskey one, are made by several companies in Ireland, although the mustard seeds are imported.

Serves 4–6

8–12 chicken joints, or 1 medium
    chicken, about 1kg/2¼lb, jointed
juice of ½ lemon
15–30ml/2–3 tbsp whiskey mustard
10ml/2 tsp chopped fresh tarragon
sea salt and ground black pepper
boiled potatoes and peas or
    mangetouts (snowpeas), to serve

1 Preheat the oven to 190°C/375°F/ Gas 5.

2 Put the chicken joints into a large shallow baking dish in a single layer and sprinkle the lemon juice over the chicken to flavour the skin.

3 Season well with sea salt and black pepper.

4 Spread the mustard over the chicken joints and sprinkle with the chopped tarragon.

5 Bake in the preheated oven for 20–30 minutes, until thoroughly cooked through.

6 Serve immediately with boiled potatoes and peas or mangetouts.

Per portion Energy 426Kcal/1768kJ; Protein 40.3g; Carbohydrate 0g, of which sugars 0g; Fat 29.3g, of which saturates 8.1g; Cholesterol 215mg; Calcium 13mg; Fibre 0g; Sodium 146mg

roast mallard

Shooting is an important Irish country pursuit and wildfowl, such as mallard, teal and widgeon, are readily available from game stores during the late autumn and early winter. Serve with game chips, apple sauce or rowan jelly, and puréed Jerusalem artichokes.

Serves 2–3

1 oven-ready mallard
1 small onion studded with about
  8 cloves
a few apple slices
25g/1oz/2 tbsp butter, softened
salt and ground black pepper
5 streaky (fatty) bacon
  rashers (strips)

1 Thoroughly wash the bird inside and out under cold running water then wipe dry on kitchen paper.

2 Weigh the mallard and calculate the cooking time at 15 minutes per 450g/1lb for rare meat, or 20 minutes per 450g/1lb if you prefer the meat well done. Preheat the oven to 200°C/400°F/Gas 6.

3 Put the onion and apple slices inside the bird. Spread the butter over the skin and season. Cover with the bacon and put into a roasting pan with 30ml/2 tbsp water.

4 Roast for the calculated time, removing the bacon for the last 10 minutes. Carve and arrange on plates, leaving the legs whole.

Per portion Energy 486Kcal/2028kJ; Protein 49.6g; Carbohydrate 0.1g, of which sugars 0.1g; Fat 32g, of which saturates 14.1g; Cholesterol 278mg; Calcium 28mg; Fibre 0g; Sodium 1.08g

braised rabbit

Rabbit now features frequently on restaurant menus. It is delicious served with potatoes boiled in their skins and a lightly cooked green vegetable.

Serves 4–6

1 rabbit, prepared and jointed by
   the butcher
30ml/2 tbsp seasoned flour
30ml/2 tbsp olive oil or vegetable oil
25g/1oz/2 tbsp butter
115g/4oz streaky (fatty) bacon
1 onion, roughly chopped
2 or 3 carrots, sliced
1 or 2 celery sticks, trimmed
   and sliced
300ml/½ pint/1¼ cups chicken stock
300ml/½ pint/1¼ cups dry (hard)
   cider or stout
a small bunch of parsley
   leaves, chopped
salt and ground black pepper
boiled potatoes and cooked
   green vegetables, to serve

1 Soak the joints in cold salted water for at least two hours, then pat them dry with kitchen paper and toss them in seasoned flour. Preheat the oven to 200°C/400°F/Gas 6.

2 Heat the oil and butter together in a heavy flameproof casserole. Shake off (and reserve) any excess flour from the rabbit joints and brown them on all sides. Lift out and set aside.

3 Add the bacon to the casserole and cook for a few minutes, then remove and set aside with the rabbit. Add the vegetables to the casserole and cook gently until just colouring, then sprinkle over any remaining seasoned flour to absorb the fats in the casserole. Stir over a low heat for 1 minute, to cook the flour. Add the stock and cider or stout, stirring, to make a smooth sauce.

4 Return the rabbit and bacon to the casserole, and add half of the chopped parsley and a light seasoning of salt and pepper. Mix gently together, then cover with a lid and put into the preheated oven.

5 Cook for 15–20 minutes, then reduce the temperature to 150°C/300°F/Gas 2 for about 1½ hours, or until tender. Add the remaining parsley and serve.

Per portion Energy 368Kcal/1535kJ; Protein 32.9g; Carbohydrate 10.5g, of which sugars 5.8g; Fat 19.7g, of which saturates 8g; Cholesterol 133mg; Calcium 88mg; Fibre 1.4g; Sodium 567mg

Dublin coddle

This traditional dish combines bacon and sausages, two foods known since the earliest Irish literature. Leeks and oatmeal were originally used with the sausages and bacon, but potatoes and onion are popular nowadays.

Makes 4 large or 8 small portions

8 x 8mm/⅓in thick ham or dry-cured bacon slices
8 best-quality lean pork sausages
4 large onions, thinly sliced
900g/2lb potatoes, peeled and sliced
90ml/6 tbsp chopped fresh parsley
salt and ground black pepper
soda bread and stout, to serve

1 Cut the ham or bacon into large chunks and cook with the sausages in 1.2 litres/2 pints/5 cups boiling water for 5 minutes. Drain, but reserve the cooking liquor.

2 Put the meat into a pan or ovenproof dish with the onions, potatoes and parsley. Season, and add just enough of the reserved liquor to cover.

3 Lay a piece of buttered foil or baking parchment on top, then add a tight-fitting lid.

4 Simmer gently for about 1 hour, or until the liquid is reduced by half and the ingredients are cooked but not mushy. Serve hot with the vegetables on top with fresh soda bread and a glass of stout.

Per portion Energy 432Kcal/1809kJ; Protein 20.6g; Carbohydrate 52g, of which sugars 10.2g; Fat 17.2g, of which saturates 6.1g; Cholesterol 45mg; Calcium 83mg; Fibre 5.7g; Sodium 1.27g

Irish stew

Ireland's national dish was traditionally made with mature mutton, but lamb is now usual. There are long-standing arguments about the correct ingredients for an authentic Irish stew apart from the meat. This is a modern variation using lamb chops.

Serves 4

1.3kg/3lb best end of neck of
    mutton (cross rib) or lamb chops,
    trimmed of fat, bone and gristle
900g/2lb potatoes
small bunch each of parsley and
    thyme, chopped
450g/1lb onions, sliced
salt and ground black pepper

1 Cut the neck meat into large pieces, if using. Slice one-third of the potatoes and cut the rest into large chunks.

2 Arrange the potatoes in a casserole, and then add herbs, half the meat and finally half the onion, seasoning each layer. Repeat, finishing with a layer of potatoes. If using chops, arrange around the edge of the pan with the onions, potatoes, herbs and seasonings in the middle.

3 Pour over 450ml/¾ pint/scant 2 cups water, and cover tightly; add a sheet of foil before putting on the lid if it is not a close-fitting one. Simmer very gently for about 2 hours, or cook in the oven at 120°C/250°F/Gas ½.

4 Check the liquid level occasionally and add extra water if necessary; there should be enough liquor to have made a gravy, thickened by the sliced potatoes.

Per portion Energy 869Kcal/3627kJ; Protein 69.1g; Carbohydrate 47.6g, of which sugars 7.7g; Fat 45.9g, of which saturates 20.8g; Cholesterol 244mg; Calcium 53mg; Fibre 4.5g; Sodium 218mg

Dingle pies

These pies are traditional in Dingle for special occasions, notably Lammas Day, 1 August, which marked the first day of the harvest. There are many recipes for mutton pies in the area, with differing ratios of meat and vegetables.

Makes 6 small pies

450g/1lb boneless mutton
  or lamb
1 large onion, diced
2 carrots, diced
1 potato, diced
2 celery sticks, diced
1 egg, beaten
salt and ground black pepper

For the shortcrust pastry

250g/9oz/generous 1 cup butter,
  or half butter and half white
  vegetable fat (shortening)
500g/1¼lb/5 cups plain
  (all-purpose) flour
120ml/4fl oz/½ cup very
  cold water

1 To make the pastry, rub the butter into the flour with the fingertips or a pastry blender. Add the chilled water. Mix with a knife or fork until the mixture clings together. Turn it on to a floured worktop and knead lightly until smooth. Wrap in foil and leave in the refrigerator to relax for 20 minutes before using.

2 Trim any fat or gristle from the meat and cut it up into small pieces. Place in a large bowl and stir in the onion, carrots, potato, celery and seasoning.

3 Preheat the oven to 180°C/350°F/Gas 4. Cut a third off the ball of pastry and reserve to make the lids of the pies. Roll out the rest and, using a small plate as a guide and re-rolling the pastry as necessary, cut out six circles. Divide the meat mixture between the circles, piling it in the middle of each.

4 Roll out the remaining pastry and cut out six smaller circles, about 10cm/4in across. Lay these on top. Dampen the edges of the pastry bases, bring the pastry up around the meat, pleat it to fit the lid and pinch the edges together.

5 Make a small hole in the top of each, brush them with beaten egg and slide on to baking sheets. Bake in the oven for an hour. Serve hot or cold.

Per portion Energy 784Kcal/3275kJ; Protein 25.1g; Carbohydrate 74.6g, of which sugars 5.2g; Fat 44.9g, of which saturates 26.1g; Cholesterol 178mg; Calcium 155mg; Fibre 4g; Sodium 345mg

beef and Guinness casserole

Stout and beef make natural partners and occur frequently in Irish cooking. This richly flavoured version of a popular dish is suitable for any occasion, including informal entertaining. Serve with creamy, well-buttered mashed potatoes.

Serves 4

900g/2lb stewing beef
30ml/2 tbsp olive oil
1 onion, chopped
2 leeks, sliced
2 carrots, sliced
2 celery sticks, sliced
2 garlic cloves, finely chopped
300ml/½ pint/1¼ cups beef stock
150ml/¼ pint/⅔ cup Guinness
50g/2oz/¼ cup butter
75g/3oz streaky (fatty) bacon
115g/4oz mushrooms, sliced
50g/2oz shallots or small onions
25g/1oz/¼ cup plain
    (all-purpose) flour
salt and ground black pepper
mashed potatoes, to serve

1 Cut the meat into thin slices. Heat the oil in a pan and brown the meat. Transfer to a casserole. Sauté the vegetables for 5 minutes in the pan.

2 Add the vegetables to the meat in the casserole, then add the garlic. Pour in the stock and the Guinness. Season with salt and ground black pepper.

3 Cover the casserole and bring to the boil, then reduce the heat and simmer, with the lid on, for about 1½ hours.

4 Remove the meat from the casserole, strain the cooking liquid and reserve. Discard the vegetables (they can be puréed with some water to make a soup).

5 Trim and dice the bacon. Clean the casserole and sauté the bacon, mushrooms and shallots or onions in the butter for 5–10 minutes.

6 When the vegetables are tender, sprinkle in the flour and cook, stirring, over a low heat for 2–3 minutes, then slowly blend in the reserved cooking liquid.

7 Return the meat to the casserole and reheat. Serve with mashed potatoes.

Per portion Energy 670Kcal/2786kJ; Protein 57.5g; Carbohydrate 14g, of which sugars 7.3g; Fat 42g, of which saturates 17.5g; Cholesterol 169mg; Calcium 71mg; Fibre 3.7g; Sodium 478mg

corned beef with dumplings and cabbage

Once the traditional favourite for Easter, corned beef now tends to be associated with St Patrick's Day. If lightly cured, the meat may need to be soaked before cooking, but check with the butcher when buying; if in doubt, soak in cold water overnight.

Serves 6

1.3kg/3lb corned silverside or brisket
1 onion, studded with 4 cloves
2 bay leaves
8–10 whole black peppercorns
1 small cabbage, finely sliced

For the dumplings
1 small onion, finely chopped
small bunch of parsley, chopped
115g/4oz/1 cup self-raising
　(self-rising) flour
50g/2oz shredded beef suet
　(US chilled, grated shortening)
salt and ground black pepper
boiled potatoes and parsley sauce

1 Soak the meat in cold water, if necessary, for several hours or overnight. When ready to cook, drain the meat and put it into a large heavy pan or flameproof casserole. Cover with fresh cold water.

2 Put the studded onion in the pan with the bay leaves and peppercorns. Bring to the boil, cover and simmer for 2 hours, until the meat is tender.

3 Meanwhile, make the dumplings: mix the onion and parsley with the flour, suet and seasoning. Add just enough water to make a soft, but not too sticky, dough. Dust your hands with flour and shape the dough into 12 small dumplings.

4 Remove the cooked meat and keep warm. Bring the cooking liquid to a boil, add the dumplings and bring back to the boil. Cover and cook for 15 minutes.

5 Meanwhile, cook the cabbage in a little of the beef stock (keep the remaining stock for making soup). Serve the beef sliced with the dumplings and shredded cabbage. Boiled potatoes and parsley sauce are traditional accompaniments.

Per portion Energy 451Kcal/1895kJ; Protein 54.6g; Carbohydrate 21g, of which sugars 4.5g; Fat 17.4g, of which saturates 7.7g; Cholesterol 139mg; Calcium 86mg; Fibre 2.4g; Sodium 142mg

side dishes

The wide range of vegetables enjoyed in Ireland today is a modern trend; most gardeners just grew simple vegetables like potatoes and cabbage (often combined to make Champ) until relatively recently. Now, however, Irish farmers, gardeners and cooks are making up for lost time and taking advantage of a surge of interest in vegetables, both traditional and more exotic, with a wealth of vivid vegetable dishes, such as Braised Swiss Chard or Baked Courgettes with Cheese.

Left: Potatoes and onions have long been staples in the Irish kitchen and are incorporated into a wide range of traditional dishes.

champ

This traditional dish of mashed potatoes flavoured with onion or herbs is especially associated with Northern Ireland. Flavourings for champ include freshly chopped chives or parsley, onions or spring onions and even green peas.

Serves 2–3

675g/1½ lb potatoes
1 bunch spring onions (scallions)
about 300ml/½ pint/1¼ cups milk
salt and ground black pepper
butter, to serve

Cook's tip

Serve as a side or main dish.

1 Peel and boil the potatoes in salted water until tender. Drain well and return to the pan.

2 Chop the spring onions, then boil for 5 minutes in the milk.

3 Cover the potatoes with a clean cloth and dry them at the side of the stove for a few minutes before mashing.

4 Beat in the milk and spring onions. Working over the heat, beat until creamy. Add more milk if necessary. Season well with pepper and salt.

5 To serve, divide the champ between heated bowls and make a well in the centre of each. Add a knob (pat) of butter. Dip the champ into the butter as you eat.

Per portion Energy 334Kcal/1415kJ; Protein 13.2g; Carbohydrate 66.6g, of which sugars 10.5g; Fat 3.5g, of which saturates 1.7g; Cholesterol 9mg; Calcium 217mg; Fibre 5.2g; Sodium 92mg

colcannon

This traditional Irish dish is especially associated with Hallowe'en, when it is likely to have a ring hidden in it – predicting marriage during the coming year for the person who found it. However, it is also served throughout the winter.

Serves 6–8

450g/1lb potatoes
450g/1lb curly kale or
   cabbage, cooked
milk, if necessary
50g/2oz/2 tbsp butter, plus extra
   for serving
1 large onion, finely chopped
salt and ground black pepper

1 Peel and boil the potatoes in salted water until tender. Drain well and return to the pan. Cover with a clean cloth and dry them at the side of the stove for a few minutes before mashing.

2 Chop the kale or cabbage, add it to the potatoes and mix. Stir in a little milk if the mash is too stiff.

3 Melt a little butter in a frying pan and add the onion.

4 Cook until softened. Remove and mix well with the potato and kale or cabbage.

5 Add the remainder of the butter to the hot pan. When very hot, turn the potato mixture on to the pan and spread it out.

6 Fry until brown, then cut it into pieces and continue frying until crisp and brown. Serve with butter.

Per portion Energy 306Kcal/1281kJ; Protein 5,4g; Carbohydrate 40.6g, of which sugars 13.6g; Fat 14.6g, of which saturates 8.8g; Cholesterol 36mg; Calcium 104mg; Fibre 5.9g; Sodium 127mg

crispy cabbage

Second only to the potato, cabbage is the most widely grown and commonly eaten vegetable in Ireland. This quick side dish makes a crunchy base for slices of boiled ham or bacon. Savoy cabbage is pretty cooked this way, as it keeps its colour.

3 Heat a wok or wide-based flameproof casserole over a fairly high heat.

4 Add the oil, heat, then add the cabbage. Stir-fry for 2–3 minutes, or until it is just cooked but still crunchy.

5 Season to taste with salt and black pepper and serve immediately.

Serves 4–6

1 medium green or
   small white cabbage
30–45ml/2–3 tbsp oil
salt and ground black pepper

1 Remove any coarse outside leaves from the cabbage. Remove the central rib from the larger remaining leaves. Shred the leaves finely.

2 Wash the cabbage thoroughly under cold running water and shake well and blot on kitchen paper to dry.

Per portion Energy 54Kcal/224kJ; Protein 1.9g; Carbohydrate 4.6g, of which sugars 4.5g; Fat 3.2g, of which saturates 0.5g; Cholesterol 0mg; Calcium 59mg; Fibre 2.7g; Sodium 6mg

braised Swiss chard

Swiss chard (also known as spinach beet) is less well known than spinach. It makes two tasty meals: on the first day, cook the leaves only; the next day cook the stalks in the same way as asparagus and serve with cream or a white sauce.

Serves 4

900g/2lb Swiss chard or spinach,
   stalks removed
15g/½oz/1 tbsp butter
a little freshly grated nutmeg
sea salt and ground
   black pepper

1 Wash the Swiss chard or spinach leaves well under cold running water and lift straight into a lightly greased heavy pan; the water clinging to the leaves will be all that is needed for cooking.

2 Cover and cook over medium heat for about 3–5 minutes, or until just tender, shaking the pan occasionally.

3 Drain well, and then add the butter and nutmeg, and season to taste with salt and black pepper.

4 When the butter has melted, toss it into the leaves and serve immediately.

Variation
Sea kale can also be cooked in the same way.

Per portion Energy 84Kcal/347kJ; Protein 6.3g; Carbohydrate 3.6g, of which sugars 3.4g; Fat 4.9g, of which saturates 2.2g; Cholesterol 8mg; Calcium 383mg; Fibre 4.7g; Sodium 338mg

baked courgettes with cheese

This easy dish makes a great accompaniment to a wide range of main courses, or it can be served with some fresh crusty bread as a light lunch or supper dish for one or two. A piquant hard cheese, such as Desmond or Gabriel, made in West Cork, will give the courgettes character, or you could use a mature farmhouse Cheddar.

3 Sprinkle the cheese over the courgettes, and top with a few knobs (pats) of butter.

4 Bake the courgettes in the preheated oven for about 20 minutes, or until they are tender and the cheese is nicely bubbling and golden brown. Serve immediately.

Serves 4

4 courgettes (zucchini)
30ml/2 tbsp grated hard farmhouse cheese, such as Gabriel, Desmond or Cheddar
about 25g/1oz/2 tbsp butter
salt and ground black pepper

1 Preheat the oven to 180°C/ 350°F/Gas 4. Slice the courgettes in half, lengthways.

2 Butter a shallow baking dish thoroughly. Arrange the courgettes, cut side up, inside the dish, with a slight space between them.

Per portion Energy 96Kcal/395kJ; Protein 3.8g; Carbohydrate 1.9g, of which sugars 1.8g; Fat 8g, of which saturates 5g; Cholesterol 21mg; Calcium 82mg; Fibre 0.9g; Sodium 93mg

baked onions

One of Ireland's oldest and most widely used flavouring vegetables, the onion also deserves to be used more as a vegetable in its own right. Onions become sweet and mildly flavoured when they are boiled or baked, and can be cooked very conveniently in the oven alongside a tray of baking potatoes or parsnips.

Serves 4

4 large even-sized onions

Cook's tip

These onions are baked in their skins, but you could peel them before baking. Cook in a covered casserole dish instead of a roasting pan.

1 Preheat the oven to 180°C/350°F/ Gas 4. Put a little cold water into a medium-size roasting pan, and arrange the unpeeled onions in it.

2 Bake in the preheated oven for about 1 hour, or until the onions feel soft when squeezed at the sides. Peel the skins and serve immediately.

Per portion Energy 90Kcal/375kJ; Protein 3g; Carbohydrate 19.8g, of which sugars 14g; Fat 0.5g, of which saturates 0g; Cholesterol 0mg; Calcium 63mg; Fibre 3.5g; Sodium 8mg

sweet treats

Memorable Irish desserts and home-baked cakes tend to be in the comfort zone – homely dishes based on simple country ingredients like home-grown apples and pears, cottage-garden summer fruits such as rhubarb, blackcurrants and strawberries, and wild berries, including blackberries and bilberries. Milk, buttermilk and cream are used in all sorts of puddings, including the much-loved Brown Bread Ice Cream, and dried fruit plays an important role in many cakes.

Left: Good home baking has always been one of the strengths of Irish cooking, and easy-to-make desserts and cakes are still very popular.

fraughan mousse

Wild or cottage-garden fruits, or a combination of both, have long been used to make simple desserts such as mousses, creams and fools. This dish made with fraughans is an attractive and impressive finish for a dinner party or special meal. Serve chilled with whipped cream and sponge fingers.

Serves 6–8

450g/1lb cooking apples
450g/1lb/4 cups fraughans (bilberries)
115g/4oz/generous ½ cup caster (superfine) sugar
juice of 1 lemon
1 sachet powdered gelatine
2 egg whites
60ml/4 tbsp double (heavy) cream, whipped, to serve

Variation

Bilberries are called fraughans in Ireland and grow prolifically in bogs and moorland areas all over Ireland in late summer. You can use other soft summer fruits, especially blueberries.

1 Peel, core and slice the cooking apples, then put them into a large pan with the fraughans, 150ml/¼ pint/⅔ cup water and 75g/3oz/scant ½ cup of the sugar. Cook gently for 15 minutes, until tender. Remove from the heat.

2 Strain the lemon juice into a cup, sprinkle the gelatine over and leave it to soak for a few minutes. Add the cake of gelatine to the fruit and stir until it has dissolved.

3 Turn the mixture into a nylon sieve (strainer) set over a large mixing bowl and press the fruit through it to make a purée; discard anything that is left in the sieve. Leave the purée to stand until it is cool and beginning to set.

4 Whisk the egg whites stiffly, sprinkle in the remaining sugar and whisk again until glossy.

5 Using a metal spoon, fold the whites gently into the fruit purée to make a smooth mousse. Turn into serving glasses and chill until set. Serve topped with whipped double cream.

 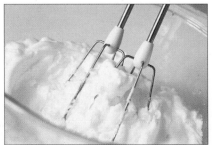 

Per portion Energy 118Kcal/498kJ; Protein 1.9g; Carbohydrate 28.7g, of which sugars 28.7g; Fat 0.2g, of which saturates 0g; Cholesterol 0mg; Calcium 44mg; Fibre 3.2g; Sodium 24mg

Bailey's carrageen pudding

Carrageen, also known as Irish moss, is a purplish variety of seaweed which is found all along the west coast of Ireland. Carrageen pudding is an old-fashioned dessert that is still widely made. This version is made with Bailey's Irish Cream and would be a good choice for a dessert selection at a party.

Serves 8–10

15g/½ oz carrageen, soaked in tepid water for 10 minutes
1.5 litres/2½ pints/6¼ cups milk
300ml/½ pint/1¼ cups Bailey's Irish Cream
2 eggs, separated
60ml/4 tbsp caster (superfine) sugar

1 Drain the carrageen and put it in a pan with the milk. Bring to the boil and simmer gently for 20 minutes, stirring occasionally.

2 Strain the mixture, rubbing all the jelly through the strainer. Rinse out the pan and return the mixture to it, over a very low heat. Blend in the Bailey's.

3 Heat the mixture gently to just below boiling point. Remove from the heat.

4 Mix the yolks and sugar together and blend in a little of the hot mixture, then whisk into the hot mixture. When the sugar has dissolved, leave to cool a little, then whisk the egg whites stiffly and fold in. Turn into dishes.

Per portion Energy 2078Kcal/8724kJ; Protein 66.3g; Carbohydrate 201.6g, of which sugars 201.6g; Fat 85.3g, of which saturates 19.8g; Cholesterol 545mg; Calcium 1.95g; Fibre 0g; Sodium 1.08g

brown bread ice cream

The secret of a good brown bread ice cream is not to have too many breadcrumbs (which makes the ice cream heavy) and, for the best texture and taste, to toast them until really crisp and well browned. Yeast bread produces a better flavour than soda bread for this recipe. Serve on its own or with a chocolate or fruit sauce.

Serves 6–8

115g/4oz/2 cups wholemeal
  (whole-wheat) breadcrumbs
115g/4oz/½ cup soft brown sugar
2 large (US extra large) eggs
30–45ml/2–3 tbsp Irish Cream liqueur
450ml/¾ pint/scant 2 cups double
  (heavy) cream

1 Preheat the oven to 190°C/375°F/ Gas 5. Spread the breadcrumbs out on a baking sheet and toast in the oven for 15 minutes, or until crisp and well browned. Leave to cool.

2 Separate the eggs. Whisk the sugar and egg yolks together until light and creamy, then beat in the Irish Cream.

3 Whisk the cream until soft peaks form. In a separate bowl, whisk the egg whites stiffly.

4 Sprinkle the breadcrumbs over the egg mixture, add the cream and fold into the mixture with a spoon. Fold in the beaten egg whites. Turn the mixture into a freezerproof container, cover and freeze.

Per portion Energy 561Kcal/2332kJ; Protein 6g; Carbohydrate 37.3g, of which sugars 23g; Fat 43.6g, of which saturates 25.7g; Cholesterol 179mg; Calcium 84mg; Fibre 0.4g; Sodium 196mg

gur cake

This spicy fruit "cake" used to be available very cheaply from Dublin bakers, who made it with their day-old bread and cakes. It is still made, although now usually sold as "Fruit Slice", and makes a delicious afternoon snack.

Makes 24 slices

8 slices of stale bread, or plain cake
75g/3oz/⅔ cup plain (all-purpose) flour
pinch of salt
2.5ml/½ tsp baking powder
10ml/2 tsp mixed (apple pie) spice
115g/4oz/generous ½ cup sugar,
    plus extra for sprinkling
175g/6oz/¾ cup mixed dried fruit
50g/2oz/¼ cup butter, melted
1 egg, lightly beaten
milk to mix

For the shortcrust pastry

225g/8oz/2 cups plain
    (all-purpose) flour
2.5ml/½ tsp salt
115g/4oz/½ cup butter

1 To make the shortcrust pastry, mix together the plain flour, salt and the butter in a large mixing bowl. Using the fingertips or a pastry blender, rub the butter into the flour until the mixture resembles fine breadcrumbs. Mix in 30–45ml/2–3 tbsp cold water and knead the mixture lightly to form a firm dough. Wrap in clear film (plastic wrap) and chill for 30 minutes.

2 Preheat the oven to 190°C/375°F/Gas 5. Grease and flour a square baking pan (tin). Remove the crusts from the bread and make the remainder into crumbs, or make the cake into crumbs.

3 Put the crumbs into a mixing bowl with the flour, salt, baking powder, mixed (apple pie) spice, sugar and dried fruit. Mix well. Add the butter and egg to the dry ingredients with enough milk to make a fairly stiff, spreadable mixture.

4 Roll out the pastry and cut out a piece to make the lid. Use the rest to line the base of the tin. Spread with the mixture, then cover with the pastry lid.

5 Make diagonal slashes across the top. Bake in the oven for 50–60 minutes, or until golden. Sprinkle with sugar and leave to cool in the tin. Cut into slices.

Per portion Energy 156Kcal/656kJ; Protein 2.4g; Carbohydrate 24.2g, of which sugars 10.5g; Fat 6.2g, of which saturates 3.7g; Cholesterol 23mg; Calcium 43mg; Fibre 0.8g; Sodium 128mg

pratie apple cake

Both sweet and savoury versions of this potato apple cake exist; this sweet one was the high point of many a farmhouse high tea, especially when using home-grown apples in autumn. At Hallowe'en it might be served instead of a Barm Brack, a traditional yeasted fruit bread, with a ring hidden inside the cake.

Serves 4–6

450g/1lb freshly cooked potatoes in their skins, preferably still warm
pinch of salt
25g/1oz/2 tbsp butter, melted
about 115g/4oz/1 cup plain (all-purpose) flour

For the filling

3 large or 4 small cooking apples, such as Bramley's Seedlings
a little lemon juice (optional)
about 50g/2oz/¼ cup butter, cut in thin slices
50–115g/2–4oz/¼ – generous ½ cup caster (superfine) sugar, or to taste

1 Preheat the oven to 200°C/400°F/Gas 6. Peel the potatoes and mash them in a large pan until smooth. Season to taste and drizzle the melted butter over.

2 Stir in as much plain flour as necessary to make a pliable dough (waxy potatoes will need more than floury ones, such as Kerr's Pink). The dough should be elastic enough to roll out, but do not knead more than necessary. Roll the mixture out into a large circle and cut into four farls (triangular pieces).

3 To make the filling, peel, core and slice the apples and pile slices of the apple on to two of the farls. Sprinkle with a little lemon juice, if you like. Dampen the edges of the farls, place the other two on top, and "nip" with your fingers around the edges to seal them together. Cook in the preheated oven for about 15–20 minutes (when the cake is nicely browned, the apples should be cooked).

4 Slit each cake around the side and turn the top back. Lay slices of butter over the apples, then sweeten with sugar. Replace the top and return to the oven until the butter and sugar have melted to make a sauce. Cut each farl into pieces and serve.

Per portion Energy 786Kcal/3307kJ; Protein 9.5g; Carbohydrate 121.9g, of which sugars 40.5g; Fat 32.4g, of which saturates 19.9g; Cholesterol 80mg; Calcium 117mg; Fibre 6.1g; Sodium 253mg

index